Ministry B

Geoff Read

Chaplain of the Anglican Church in Basel, Switzerland

GROVE BOOKS LIMITED

RIDLEY HALL RD CAMBRIDGE CB3 9HU

Contents

Acknowledgments

My sincere thanks to all who supported me through my own burnout episode, especially my wonderful wife and daughters. Thanks too to those who have generously offered advice and materials to me in writing this booklet.

First Impression December 2009
ISSN 0144-171X
ISBN 978 1 85174 742 9

1 Introduction

In mid 2004 I sat in a meeting and found myself asking trusted clergy colleagues, 'When is enough, enough?' Their loving concern triggered a process that led to my doctor writing me off from work suffering from depression. It was the first time that anything like this had happened to me. I was both grateful for being able to name the disorder and also uncomfortable with the diagnosis; not because of any stigma but because it seemed to tell only part of the story. My psychiatrist subsequently offered a wider framework for understanding what was happening: burnout. This embraced the symptom of depression but set it and me in the wider context of my whole life, and in particular my work as an Anglican minister. I instinctively felt that this role—my understanding of it and the work associated with it—was also a contributory factor, even though it is something that I have always loved and rejoiced in ever since my ordination.

I decided to embrace the diagnosis as an opportunity. My recovery included the contribution of family, friends and church community, local and diocesan. It was a privilege to be treated by an excellent Christian psychotherapist. In addition I was supported by a spiritual director who gently guided me to reconnect with questions about my identity—'Who does God say I am?', 'Who do I say he is?' A mentor completed the team, building on my fresh insights into identity with questions about purpose: 'Why do you do what you do?' 'For what are you truly responsible and why?'

In addition I felt the need to understand this thing called burnout. How can sincere, motivated, competent clergy find themselves at this point? I began to read and research burnout in relation to the ordained and other 'professional Christians.' As I recognized the signs in myself I became alarmed at what I saw in others. While mercifully few go on to an episode of burnout, many, I suspect, linger just above it, coping with the demands of ministry and robbed of its joys.

Many linger just above burnout, coping with the demands of ministry and robbed of its joys

Much has been written recently about clergy stress and burnout. In the UK this includes the excellent report *Affirmation and Accountability* by the Society of Mary and Martha, while from the USA the work of Roy Oswald and the Alban Institute is very accessible and helpful.[1]

Particular mention must be made of the work of Professor Leslie Francis, who has carried out specialist academic research about how personality, context, personal, family and ministry factors contribute to clergy stress and burnout. Writing in the UK, and largely published only in academic journals, his extensive research has been carried out among a variety of denominations and in several English-speaking countries. In the course of his research he has developed two important tools. The first is the Francis Burnout Inventory, a development of the Maslach Burnout Inventory adapted to reflect the language and experience of parochial clergy, and the other is the Francis Psychological Type Scales. The Francis Burnout Inventory was used in two major pieces of work in 2004 among Church of England and Roman Catholic clergy that were reported widely in the church press.

Alongside this excellent scientific research this booklet offers two contributions: a personal perspective; and highlighting the issue of identity in relation to burnout. The personal aspect includes not only my own experience but also conversations with other clergy and full-time Christian workers. The focus on the importance of a dynamic, growing and renewed identity in Christ may seem obvious. But often the important gives way to the urgent, the good forces out the best. I hope that honesty about my own experience of unintentional neglect might stimulate others to reflect about and to act on this most important foundational element in ministry.

Chapter two offers an overview of the phenomenon of burnout, followed by theological reflection on identity and role in chapter three. The practical suggestions for healthy engagement with ministry in chapter four focus on disciplines related to identity.

Questions for Reflection

- How do you react emotionally to the term burnout?
- Can you conceive of it happening to you?
- What do you think of those who have experienced it?

Burnout: A Multifaceted Syndrome

2

Burnout has become a popularized term to cover a response of exhaustion to various demanding life contexts, in particular work. Rather than a distinct illness, it is a syndrome in which a number of factors and disorders come together including, for example, depression and anxiety-related disorders. Treatment of the individual components of burnout could include psychotherapy, medication, spiritual direction and mentoring.

Burnout was a term first coined in 1974 by Freudenberger in *Burnout: The High Cost of High Achievement*.[2] This was followed by the highly influential work of Christina Maslach, Professor of Psychology at the University of California, starting with *Burnout: The Cost of Caring*.[3] Out of this she developed the Maslach Burnout Inventory (MBI), which addresses three dimensions:

Emotional Exhaustion

You feel drained and lack the mental or physical energy to get on with whatever you need to do: lack of creativity; 'It can't be Sunday again already…'; a lack of pleasure in daily life; 'things will never change…'; agitation; irritation and outbursts of anger; broken sleep patterns; physical exhaustion; inability to concentrate.

Detachment

An increasingly strong negative, hostile, cynical, dehumanized response to your role in general and everyone who is part of it: '… not her again…'; less time with people, more at the computer; avoiding personal encounters; taking refuge behind the clerical collar; escape into comfort-eating or drinking; day dreaming and inattention to 'now.'

Sense of Lack of Achievement

You develop a negative sense of who you are and what you are doing: running a church rather than ministry; reactive rather than proactive; inefficient desk-work; procrastination; 'why him and not me…'; desperation; 'how can I have reached this point?'

Building on Maslach's work, Leslie Francis has helpfully highlighted how these three dimensions combine in a subtle way. Together they represent degrees of negative and positive effect. So, for example, someone may experience emotional exhaustion and yet be able to remain relatively healthy psychologically due to a high degree of sense of achievement. It is when the high degree of negative effect (emotional exhaustion) combines with a low degree of positive effect (sense of achievement) that burnout can occur.

Burnout, Stress and Other Disorders

The term 'burnout' is frequently used in everyday language interchangeably with 'stress.' A more precise use of both terms is needed in order to address adequately each of these different but related phenomena.

Stress is essentially the physiological or psychological response to many different sorts of situations and demands. Stress becomes distress when the stress is of a particular nature, intensity, duration or frequency. Burnout is one response to sustained exposure to certain sorts of stressors.

A person reaches a state of burnout when the three factors of emotional exhaustion, detachment and sense of lack of achievement have reached a level of such severity that the person's ability to function is significantly impaired. These three factors are not unique to burnout but can also be experienced during depression and other disorders.

Central in burnout is the person's experience of the workplace, namely the way their identity and purpose shapes their interpretation of this domain of their lives. As they experience stressors in the workplace they (mis)interpret that experience based on their presuppositions, previous experience and personality. Such misinterpretation will be explored in this booklet in relation to burnout and Christian ministry.

Burnout Can Happen to All Sorts of People

A common perception of burnout is that it only happens to 'weak' people. However, many who reach latter stages of burnout are there because of the misplaced use of qualities such as tenacity and dedication and a strong sense of responsibility to reach goals. It can affect different personality types for different reasons. So it is better to say that burnout happens to people with certain sorts of weaknesses or at certain moments of weakness.

For example, for some it can arise from having only 24 hours in a day and the competing roles of, for example, church and home. Equally, this can develop from the disconnect between the glowing expectations of what we believe ministry ought to look like and its everyday reality. Sheer volume can also be the stressor for the others who feel compelled to 'fix and please.' More significant for them, though, can be the stress of meeting the competing expectations of what others think church and ministry should look like. Vulnerability in squaring those competing and mismatching expectations includes perfectionism, lack of differentiation, co-dependency and lack of realistic expectations. Roland Croucher suggest that the mismatches are '... usually something to do with family-of-origin deficits in terms of unconditional love, a sense of belonging, and a tendency towards competitiveness to prove one's worth.'[4]

Leslie Francis' research points to personality being the strongest predictor of burnout. In the two studies of 2004 among Anglican and Roman Catholic clergy, Francis used a three-dimensional model of personality in which each dimension lies along a spectrum: Extraversion (introversion to extraversion); Neuroticism (emotional stability to emotional instability); and Psychoticism (tender mindedness to tough mindedness to psychotic disorder). He looked at the correlation between these three dimensions of personality and the three dimensions of burnout: emotional exhaustion; detachment; and a sense of lack of achievement. The research drew attention to '...the centrality of extraversion and of neuroticism in predicting clergy susceptibility to burnout... Put crudely, neurotic introverts are much more likely to become victims of burnout than stable extroverts, and this holds true across a range of different ministry contexts.'[5]

Once identified, acknowledged and addressed, the awareness of personality factors can become a potential asset rather than, when unacknowledged, a potential liability. The sooner these dispositions to burnout are identified the better, so that they can become a conscious focus in initial and ongoing formation in the individual during training for ordained ministry (*Affirmation and Accountability*, 2.3.2).

Burnout is Not Just About the Individual

Over the years Christiana Maslach has come to give ever greater weight in her work to the variables of the workplace context alongside those of personality. 'Burnout reflects an uneasy relationship between people and their work...a bad fit...rather than just individual weaknesses, or just evil workplaces.'[6] Mismatch is essentially about the gap between expectations and reality and Maslach believes that this mismatch can happen in any of six areas:

- the imbalance of workload and resources
- the degree of meaningful control one exercises
- fair reward, recognition and satisfaction
- community dynamics
- fairness of treatment by superiors
- values, the sense of one's work making a difference

While arising from extensive research in the secular workplace, Maslach's six areas can easily be translated into the church context. For example, the mismatch of workload can be seen in the relentless regrouping of parishes in the face of declining clergy numbers without the strategic help and development necessary to make this change. In the area of meaningful control one characteristic in particular stands out: role ambiguity. This ranges, for example, from the frequent absence of a job description to the lack of clarity about where accountability lies to the strange lack of handover processes between successive incumbents. In church life, the area of fair reward may be less about actual pay and more about the lack of 'strokes' due to the hidden and confidential nature of much pastoral ministry. This area also relates to the current shift in many denominations towards a human resources/employment dynamic in care of clergy, the flat career path and limited opportunities for the recognition and sharing of experience.[7] Community dynamics can include the stresses of a particular parish such as location (inner city or rural ministry), isolation, conflict and church size transitions.[8] One obvious characteristic in this category is the nature of ongoing pastoral encounters when such encounters are direct, frequent and problem focused, particularly when dealing with chronic issues. In the sixth category, value mismatch can arise simply but very significantly in the ongoing gap between the ideal of the Body of Christ and the day-to-day realities of life in a local church.

If both the individual and organization share in creating the circumstances in which burnout can occur, they must both share in reversing the process through what Maslach calls 'engagement.' This is not just practical fixing but more about questioning and renegotiating the mismatched presuppositions and conditions in each area. It is important for the individual to consider their contribution to the mismatch so that even in the face of denial by the local church or denomination, individuals can reframe their presuppositions and try new patterns. Eventually they might decide that the only response to the degree and cost of the mismatch is to leave a post.

Burnout and Working Too Hard and Too Long

Long-hours culture is certainly both a symptom and contributory cause of burnout. However, if burnout is essentially about one's interpretation of stress, a more fruitful area of investigation is to ask qualitative questions. Protracted exposure to others' suffering can lead to compassion fatigue. But burnout is not limited to just those in the traditional helping professions such as education, healthcare and ordained ministry as early research originally suggested.

In a fascinating *New Yorker* magazine article, 'Can't Get No Satisfaction' (November 2006), Jennifer Senior writes of the burnout experienced by Wall Street bankers under the provocative subtitle, 'In a culture where work can be a religion, burnout is its crisis of faith.' The common thread between the experiences of this group and some clergy is not just long hours worked but the perceived lack of fulfilment, albeit of very different sorts. This focuses on the apparent gap between the motivating expectations and the reality experienced. Be it the expectation of exponential stockmarket growth for a perfectionist stockbroker or the expectations of signs of fulfilment in kingdom ministry for conscientious clergy, the perceived gap can be a significant contributory factor to burnout. So how do we learn to understand and to respond to the gap?

The recognition of the systemic factors of the workplace are a welcome addition to those of personality in burnout thinking. If thinking is to be truly holistic, then two further factors need to be considered: private and family life; and wider health. The Swiss Christian psychiatrist, Samuel Pfeifer, notes the 'spill-over effect' between the stresses of work and private life. Quoting research by Lask, 63% of respondents admitted to significant spill-over from family stress into the workplace.[9]

But stress is not only a cause of health issues; it can also be a consequence. Pfeifer points out how illness or injury affects one's confidence as the reliable given of a healthy body comes into question. This raises important practical and spiritual questions about the neglect of the body by many clergy through the failure to eat, exercise and rest properly. My body is not just a machine to move me around my ministry context. It is a part of who I am, to be cherished and honoured.

Burnout May Be Related to Particular Points in Ministry

In 1999 a major study into burnout was carried out among clergy in the US Lutheran Missouri Synod (*Clergy Shortage Study*, Klaas and Klaas) that suggested burnout was a problem at a mid-point in life or in a life-long ministry. The study estimated that 40% of all pastors in the Synod were experiencing mild to severe burnout. A 2002 study by Austin Presbyterian Theological Seminary tracked graduates for seven years after graduation, finding that younger or more recently ordained clergy were not experiencing burnout in their initial years of incumbency. In contrast, in a Commission on Urban Life and Faith work group on clergy stress, Leslie Francis suggested that younger or more recently appointed incumbents were perceived to be at greater risk, while older or longer-serving ones 'had developed a strategy to deal with it.'[10] He concluded in a later study (2004) that none of the three dimensions of burnout are related to length of time in the present appointment.

From my own experience and observation I believe that factors can combine to create a greater vulnerability to burnout at particular stages of life and ministry for some clergy. By ministry, that includes not only overall length of ministry but also time in a particular context. This is not only due to sustained exposure to the particular pressures of that context but also the internal dynamics of the developing pastor-congregation relationship. For example, Israel Galindo calls year seven in a parish the year of 'recharge or burnout,' urging clergy to remember the value of sabbatical and the principles behind it.[11]

Burnout is a Process Rather Than a Crisis

Unlike depression which, if not endogenous, is a reaction to a crisis, burnout is a process with recognized stages that lead to a point of crisis. My own psychiatrist described it as like successive steps down into a dark cellar. The way back from burnout is to reverse those steps.

> Burnout doesn't just happen from one day to the next. Most experience a gradual increase in symptoms, knocking quietly on the door, withdrawing slightly at (times of rest), until they finally break in with an intensity like a thunderbolt... (Pfeiffer)

Dr John Fletcher's *Clergy Burnout Cycle* outlines seven steps in this journey. Entry to ordained ministry with high personal ideals is overlaid with those of the church during training (1).[12] Once in a post, ideal and contextual reality disconnect and clergy draw ever deeper on the ideal, propelled by a growing sense of 'ought' (2). The demands and the disconnect lead to symptoms of physical, relational and spiritual stress (3). By step 4 the route of an individual's response to this stress has divided between those for whom it is episodic and who will cope and those who are on the road to burnout as quiet despair sets in. This is followed by the emergence of cynicism and resentment towards the perceived demands of church members or clients, and diminished creativity (5). In steps 6 and 7 the horror at such feelings is turned inwards and the individual either crumbles at this stage or dedicates him- or herself to trying harder while achieving less and less, delaying the inevitable crash. Treatment initially involves the removal of the immediate pressure, allowing the retracing of these steps.

Burnout, Time Management and Work-life Balance

Improved competence in time management and work-life balance will help, but they really only address symptoms of burnout rather than the core problem. What is needed is to dig deep to the spiritual and theological issue of identity: 'How do I see God; how does he see me?' 'How do I see the world and how does the world see me?' How we answer these questions shapes our engagement with God and the world; the issue of purpose.

For clergy and other 'professional Christians' these questions are often confused by a lack of clear statements of purpose and parameters, both within and between the various roles they have in their professional and personal lives. This is particularly so for clergy who often lack clear job descriptions. Knowing why I do what I do based on concrete, objective and theologically rooted imperatives is essential for avoiding burnout. Tools that equip us to be reflective practitioners are equally, if not more, important than those of time management.

Is Burnout Honourable?

'Better to burn out than to rust out.' I have personally never heard anyone actually say such a thing, but I have seen attitudes and lifestyles that communicate it. Superficially, such an attitude communicates commitment and dedication. But is this really what God desires and requires of us? How does that square with the invitation to share with Jesus his easy yoke (Mt 11.28–30)? What picture of God and of human beings does 'burning out' communicate?

Rather than a sign of virtue, burnout may be recognized as an unwitting sin of omission. In *A Long Obedience in the Same Direction,* Eugene Peterson quotes the warning of Hilary of Tours: *Irreligiosa sollicitudo pro Deo,* a blasphemous anxiety to do God's work for him. The shift from 'working with' to 'working for,' from God-sufficiency to well-meaning self-sufficiency, is a very subtle but significant one. It is also a very easy shift for highly committed and motivated Christians, seeking to serve God's kingdom in slow-moving and apparently unpromising contexts.

Whether you burn out or rust out you are still 'out.' Surely what is needed is that we burn on in a healthy and sustainable ministry and life, something that lies in an ever-deepening grasp of our true identity in Christ. A prayer of St Ignatius Loyola catches the balance of freedom in Christ and the shift to willing and costly servanthood. Loyola was someone who understood, *par exellence,* how to read the movements of the human heart. Without that deepening identity of freedom in Christ the prayer is a frightening recipe for burnout but, with it, a description of perfect freedom.

> Lord, teach me to be generous.
> Teach me to serve you as you deserve;
> to give and not to count the cost,
> to fight and not to heed the wounds,
> to toil and not to seek for rest,
> to labour and not to ask for reward,
> save that of knowing that I do your will.
>
> St Ignatius Loyola (1491–1556)

How do you read this prayer—as a call to obligation or an expression of freedom?

You Can Recover From Burnout

The cost of burnout to the individual, their immediate family and friends, church community and denomination can be enormous (*Affirmation and Accountability*, 1.5). This is emotional, practical and financial. The sooner the route towards burnout is recognized the greater the possibility of recovery. Depending on the severity of the burnout, if that recovery is to be one aimed at avoiding future relapses it must involve a commitment to an intentional and often long process. For most who experience burnout it is possible to resume roles gradually, hopefully with deepened personal insight into themselves and those roles and with strategies for anticipating and responding to future warning bells. This, indeed, was my own experience.

At the beginning my doctor insisted on reducing my workload to 50%. Encouraged by the local church leadership I focused on those things that I would enjoy and find energizing. This included regular Sunday preaching and also continuing pastoral accompaniment of a young woman who was terminally ill. We also agreed that I should relinquish completely day-to-day church responsibilities and decision-making. That was not easy but proved to be a vital first step. With the benefits of psychotherapy, spiritual direction and mentoring I gradually recovered and was able to increase my workload back to 100% through carefully planned and agreed steps over a total of nine months.

But what is the nature of this recovery for the individual—healing or managing a vulnerability? Where burnout has been embraced by the individual as an invitation to growth in identity and purpose, how will others perceive it? In particular, how will it be treated by denominations ever more human resources-orientated in relation to selection, appointment and pensions and therefore, maybe, ever more risk-averse? I asked someone in the Church of England central structures this question: 'As someone who has grown through burnout, am I regarded as an asset or a liability?' He replied, 'It all depends…'!

For Reflection

Pause and fill in the Burnout Indicator in Appendix 1.

As you reflect on the results ask yourself the following questions:
- How vulnerable to burnout do I currently feel?
- What might make me vulnerable in the future?
- Are those personal factors or contextual ones?
- How might I begin to address them?

Identity and Role

3

Identity

Our identity in Christ is a root issue for all Christians, not just clergy. But the representative dimension of priesthood and profile of other 'professional Christians' does mean that any deficits will be under particular and sustained pressure. The way that Jesus' own ministry began is highly significant and instructive following the pattern of identity, vocation and only then ministry. His baptism is first and foremost affirmation of his identity by the Father as 'My Son whom I love' (Lk 3.23). In obedience to the Spirit he is led into the desert where, in temptation about that identity, clarity about his vocation is gained. He then returns to Galilee '...in the power of the Spirit' (Lk 4.14) and ministry begins. Jesus' daily ministry began with immersion in this pattern as he rose early to be in prayer with his Father, celebrating and revelling in that identity. Out of this secure place he was clear about his own vocation and the way that found expression in the choices of daily life and ministry (John 5.19).

In his book, *Fifty Rituals for Life,* the German Benedictine theologian Anselm Gruen draws attention to a further dimension of Jesus' identity through words he uses post-resurrection in Luke 24.39.[13] Following his hiddenness and self-disclosure on the Emmaus road as Jesus then appears in the upper room he says, 'It is I myself' (*ego eimi autos*). Gruen points out that the Greek word *autos* has particular significance, meaning '...the inner holiness of the person, the inner core, the real self.' Slightly provocatively he then continues, 'In the resurrection Jesus has become his real self' (p 140). This is our aim as the resurrection touches our lives, the process of life-long transformation. As these words of Jesus progressively become our own, Gruen comments, we become '...authentic, self-sufficient, genuine and free' (p 141, my translation).

From my own experience I describe burnout as the chronic stress of trying to square the circle of other people's expectations about who I am and what I do. Among those others is God too. Without a clear sense of identity and purpose, clergy are subject to the stress of either the chronic effort to fulfil those expectations—acting like a plate spinner dashing to keep numerous plates in the air—or living with

Burnout is the chronic stress of trying to square the circle of other people's expectations

the chronic pain of never truly being themselves—like a left-handed person forced to write with the right hand. But why do individuals choose to live this way? Is the drivenness of burnout that comes from people-pleasing and misplaced God-pleasing an unwitting act of practical atheism, a denial of the grace of God?

An important part of prevention and recovery lies in embracing the basic call of the kingdom: to repent (Mt 4.17) in the sense of to change, to turn around. The changing and renewing of our minds involved in this is not just about ourselves, but about our image of God too. One of the most powerful of the kingdom parables that deal with this double change of mind in relation to identity is that of the lost son (Lk 15.11–32).

A Model for Our Identity by Henri Nouwen: As a Child of God

As I read Nouwen's *The Return of the Prodigal Son* during my own burnout I did not realize, at the time, why I found it so helpful.[14] Only subsequently did I discover that *The Return* is the public and safe place for insights gained during Nouwen's own burnout-like episode during the first six months of 1988. Only at a later date did he agree to the publication of his private journal of that period as *The Inner Voice of Love.*[15]

Nouwen asks of the sons: if 'home' is the place where we are perfectly known and loved by the Father, why do we, as human beings, feel the need to go elsewhere to find that love? For Nouwen, the key lies in accepting our true identity as a child of God. 'Once you have claimed it and settled in it, you can live in a world that gives you much joy as well as pain' (*The Inner Voice of Love,* p 70).

Perhaps most telling in the context of clergy burnout is the eldest son, the one who stays behind to do the right thing, but in his heart has wandered away from his father and from home just as surely as his younger brother. His cry to the father says it all: 'All these years I've been slaving for you…' (Lk 15.29). He has the status of son but the experience of slave. The father's response is highly significant: whether he realizes it or not, the son is always with him and all that the father has is his.

Both sons struggle with their true identity in their different ways and for different reasons. Nouwen calls the path to acceptance '…allowing ourselves to be fully received' by God's unconditional love. Without it, there is great danger '…in pouring yourself out to others in the hope they will fully receive you. You will soon feel as though others are walking away with parts of you. You cannot give to others if you do not own yourself' (*The Inner Voice of Love,* p 65).

A Model of Identity by Wendell Friest: As a Voluntary Slave or Servant of God

In his work on burnout originally addressed to OMF missionaries, Dr Wendell Friest describes two distinct missionary types.[16] Type A is characterized by a sense of self worth and self-acceptance based on achievement. Type B finds identity in giving and meeting the needs of others. Both lead to driven lives that Friest characterizes as achievement fatigue (Type A) and compassion fatigue (Type B). Like Nouwen, Friest believes that reconnecting with the freedom that is rooted in our identity in Christ is a crucial resource for the Christian in combating burnout, for both Type A and B temperaments. This involves not just the theological but also experiential movement from slave to sin, to son/daughter of God, and then on to a freely chosen slavery or servanthood.

The heart of the good news is the restoration of God the Father's original purposes for his children: the status of sonship rather than slavery (Gal 4.4–7). But, so often, experience lags behind the theological reality and so acceptance and identity can remain rooted in slavery or addiction to achievement or meeting others' expectations. Burnout can be not only a result of such slavery but also a key opportunity to face this disconnect between what we preach and what we experience. Burnout can become an invitation to connect experientially with the transforming power of grace in terms of our identity. Freedom simply to 'be' replaces the drive to have to 'do' to prove something (Type A) or assuage the guilt of being unable to fulfil all the needs of others (Type B). This newfound freedom finds expression in ministry, enabling one '...to get back into the slave modality without losing the son-daughter modality.' Friest calls this Slave Modality 2, what I prefer to call servanthood. In Christ we see this voluntary self-emptying as described in Philippians 2.5–11. Paul's prized status as 'slave' (1 Cor 9.19) is one he freely adopts. It is clear from Romans 12.1 that this is a voluntary decision on the part of the individual, a free response to God's merciful adoption of us as sons and daughters.

The heart of the good news is the restoration of the Father's original purposes for his children

Friest comments, 'If we are slaves to God unwillingly, because we feel this is God's demand, something he has imposed or exacted, there will never be joy in our lives—only complaining (maybe repressed), resentment, and bitterness... [But] in being both a child of God and a slave of God we are identifying with Jesus. We are free "to be abased, and...to abound" (Phil 4.12).' We can enjoy life without guilt, and we can serve without drivenness or compulsion, and without a need for achievement or recognition.

Both models of identity also invite conscious reconnecting with the one who calls and, prior to that, who simply loves us. This is a spirituality that is relational, about me as me rather than just me as a minister. What is my God like? Have I unconsciously distorted my perception of him too? Is there a disconnect between the God of grace I say I believe in and proclaim and the image of him that I actually live and take into my vocation and on into my functioning in ministry? Allowing God to be God to us enables a growing experience of one's identity in Christ to re-emerge. This is rooted in grace and unconditional love rather than just existing with an identity dependent on performance and the opinion of others.

Role

Clarity about one's purpose is equally vital for such a ministry. What am I really called to be and do? This clarity involves the interaction of: my agreed role; my unique combination of gifts, competencies and experience (Me); and the particularities of my context.[17]

Being able to answer the vocational question, 'Why do I do what I do?' is essential, in turn, for being able to make meaningful decisions about use of time in the how and what of ministry. It empowers clergy to shift from a reactive ministry, driven by the expectations and demands of others, to one that is proactive, intentional and driven by conviction. Three areas merit particular attention in relation to burnout: the gap between desired and actual reality; conflict and criticism; and ambiguity of role.

Living With the Gap

While all Christians live with the gap between the fullness of the reality in which we believe and life here and now, this gap can be experienced particularly acutely by clergy in relation to the church. The context and content of their work and the message they are called to proclaim often keeps this gap or mismatch firmly before their eyes. In addition, Fletcher's Burnout Cycle (see chapter two) describes how responsibility for the gap can be personally assumed.

All Christians live with the gap between the fullness of the reality in which we believe and life here and now

One key resource in living with the ambiguities of ministry is a conscious awareness of the 'now but not yet' nature of the kingdom. In addition, it is God's kingdom built through his initiative (Mark 4.26–29) and in ways that need to be understood from the perspective of the cross rather than the world. And even though the kingdom creates the church, the church is not the kingdom. Reflecting on the parable of the net (Mt 13.47–50) which likens the action of the kingdom to drawing a net through the sea, G E Ladd comments that, 'The empirical church has a twofold character. It is the people of the kingdom, and yet it is not the ideal people, for it includes some who are actually not sons of the kingdom' (*The Presence of the Future*, p 265). Even those who are, are saints in the making!

Living with Conflict and Criticism

The minister is often at the centre of criticism and conflict resolution. It is clear that some personality types are naturally more suited to dealing with conflict, while for others it is a question of consciously acquiring attitudes and skills of '...hardiness and resilience' (*Affirmation and Accountability*, 2.3.1).

Every human organization and its leadership has to deal with conflict and criticism. However, there are particular and complicating dynamics at play in churches. Unlike in the clearer parameters of the paid workplace, the voluntary nature of the local church can significantly skew the handling of conflict and criticism. Other dynamics include, for example, a latent ambivalence about how conflict should be handled, confidentiality, the diversity of deeply held preferences and convictions and, last but not least, the knock-out argument of a claim to divine guidance!

The voluntary nature of the local church can skew the handling of conflict and criticism

The biblically motivated shift towards empowered lay ministry has brought with it a change in the role of the ordained minister as will be explored in the next section. This has coincided with a wider development in society away from trust and respect for authority figures. In addition the increased financial responsibility by local churches for clergy pensions and stipends has stirred an increasing sense of congregationalism. With this comes the expectation of accountability from an ever-wider range of people, whether that is a correct and fair expectation or not.

Living With Ambiguity of Role

Ambiguity of role is not just about the lack of clear job descriptions or terms and conditions. In his book, *Ministry in Three Dimensions,* Steven Croft highlights the wider issue of the increasing importance in recent years of the *episcope* or oversight dimension of all ordained ministry. In addition to those associated with pastoral service, the cure of souls and the worshipping life of the church this dimension requires competency in the areas of leadership and team development to best enable the ministry of the whole people of God. However, he observes that, '[For] much of the twentieth century the Church of England has trained curates in its theological colleges and courses, not incumbents.'[18] In addition, those from this group, who are now incumbents, are leading at a time of transition in what it means to be church, simultaneously looking back to inherited mode and forward to emerging mode.

Leadership is now a welcome part of selection for ordination, initial (IME) and continuing ministerial education (CME). In addition, steps are being taken to address this deficit for current incumbents who received little training in leadership, including, for example, *The Leadership Programme,* which since 2001 has been offered in nine Church of England dioceses. In addition, since its introduction to the UK in 1999 by CPAS, over two hundred church leaders have benefited from the *Arrow Leadership* programme.[19] Impressive as this is, it still covers a relatively small number of the current generation of longer standing incumbents. For the rest, 'winging it' in this increasingly important area of oversight can only be, for the most part, a considerable source of stress.

> Preserve me from my calling's snare,
> and hide my simple heart above,
> above the thorns of choking care,
> the gilded baits of worldly love.
>
> *Forth in Thy name,* v 3
> Charles Wesley (1749)

For Reflection

- Which aspects of your role are, for you, 'my calling's snare'?
- How does lack of clarity about your role contribute to that?
- What practical difference would it make to have greater clarity in that area and how could you achieve that?

Engagement: Preventing Clergy Burnout

4

Maslach's recent work has started to focus on the positive antithesis of burnout: engagement.[20] I find this a helpful and positive term that describes exactly the process I went through and in which I find myself today.

Engagement suggests meaningful and intentional dialogue, investment of effort in order to attain a positive outcome. It is a term that describes the steps that can be taken in addressing burnout by an individual and an organization, both the intrapersonal and contextual aspects. Engagement has practical outcomes through changed attitudes and awareness and particular concrete practices. It also describes the ongoing effort needed to pursue the positive match between the individual and the work beyond a burnout episode. In other words, engagement enables highly motivated, competent and sincere individuals to thrive throughout a lifelong ministry.

In this final chapter I want to continue to focus on identity and point to areas for further thought for individuals and the church that could help to prevent burnout.

Engagement Through a Commitment to Personal Development and Ministry-long Learning

For the Individual

At the heart of personal development for any Christian is a commitment to a developing spirituality. The experience of our true identity is found particularly in prayer of a contemplative nature. In his short but rich and perceptive book on leadership, *Hit the Ground Kneeling*, Stephen Cottrell calls this, 'Letting the grass grow under our feet.' 'Reclaiming this first love can be one of the best ways of renewing our energy for leadership…'[21] Making such prayer a regular discipline is a vital foundation for fulfilling, effective and sustainable ministry.

But ironically this can be the area of greatest struggle for many clergy and others in full-time ministry. Chris Edmonson offers a wider discussion of personal strategies for sustaining healthy ministry in *Minister—Love Thyself! Sustaining Healthy Ministry* (Grove Pastoral booklet P 83), which has at its heart developing a personal spirituality rooted in being rather than action.

While personal development can take many forms, in relation to identity it starts with a commitment to a growing sense of self-knowledge. The importance of this for clergy is highlighted by the conclusions of Leslie Francis that personality type is a primary indicator in predicting burnout. His research shows that the majority of Church of England clergy are of a more introverted personality type but engaged in a role with strong extrovert demands. Such individuals need to address what this awareness means in terms of patterns of daily ministry with adequate time for recovery and ways of finding satisfaction through more introverted tasks.[22]

But in order to be able to grow you need to have some means of identifying where you are at, of taking stock. Sometimes we have the bare bones of the information for such insight scattered around us—from courses or a previously administered psychometric test, feedback from a spiritual director, a spouse. But it can be worthwhile to seek out a structured test with a report and feedback from a trained practitioner. The popular Myers-Briggs Personality Indicator can yield enormous insights that can set you off on growth in relation to spirituality, teamwork, relationships and decision-making style. A more recent and increasingly popular tool is the Personal Ecology Profile of the Leadership Community.[23]

- What am I prepared to do to grow as a person?
- What resources do I currently have that can help me to understand myself better?
- What resources could I invest in?

Engagement is also about adopting a longer-term perspective on professional development. While annual in-service training courses can offer vital short-term, skills-based development, the longer-term perspective is found in the realm of sabbatical and post-graduate courses in various areas of applied theology. The latter, taken at the right point in ministry, can have the very positive effect of allowing structured critical reflection and the integration of the gap between theory and practice.

For the Church

Leslie Francis' conclusions that personality factors provide a better prediction of burnout than personal, contextual, family or ministry factors raise important questions for selection, formation and support of those called to ordained ministry.

How might a more rigorous use of psychological testing at selection and during formation at theological college serve as a foundation for developing the resilience needed for a lifelong ministry? In a few cases the mismatch between the individual and the role is too great and an individual ought not to be recommended for training. But for all others the insights of such testing could become the subject of intentional engagement, a central part of the formation process throughout initial and continuing ministerial education, as recommended by both Francis and the Sheldon Report, *Affirmation and Accountability* (2.3.2).

Engagement Through Maximizing the Match Between Clergy and Their Ministry Context

For the Individual

An important aspect of personal awareness is also about preferred or natural styles of working including leadership, working in a team, handling stress and decision-making. The need to operate for a sustained period outside these preferred styles can be a source of increased stress. An individual can engage with any reasonable mismatch by either training or the composition of a team of which they are a part. Adequate and appropriate support is also crucial as explored in *Finding Support in Ministry* (Grove Pastoral booklet P 90), a series of short essays edited by Nick Helm and Philip Allin.

For the Church

Affirmation and Accountability stresses the value of psychometric tools in 'fitting the right clergy to the right kind of job where they can flourish and work most effectively' (2.3.2). This matching is surely a dynamic process in terms of both clergy and parishes and involves not just the appointment itself but also the first year of the relationship and subsequent key transitions. Roy Oswald of the Alban Institute points to the importance of laying good foundations of mutual expectation before an appointment and the value of external coaching during the first year.[24] For example, the Canadian Brian Fraser's *Starting Smart* coaching programme accompanies ministers new to a post in exploring their own and the church's inner resources, culture and team dynamics and helps to set a mutually agreed new learning agenda.[25] Such insights in preventing burnout could be equally important for both clergy and the churches they lead at other key transition points where mismatches are liable to occur.

Engagement Through Reflection on the Important

For the Individual

In *First Things First*, Steven Covey identifies 'first things' as those things for an individual which are not only significant in the execution of their duties but also which bring a deep sense of satisfaction in relation to their values and gifts.[26] When we are able regularly and intentionally to factor into our schedules those non-urgent and important things, we are not only most effective but also most alive. This is the realm of vocation and it is something that, hopefully, need not only be limited to work but to the whole of life. Awareness of what is truly important emerges from intentional reflection on what one wants to be and do, expressed in a personal and unique mission statement.[27]

One of the most significant questions I was asked by my mentor during my recovery from burnout was, 'For what do you feel responsible?' I can laugh at the response now, but it was not funny then: everything! Out of this question emerged a process of defining what is truly important in my life in general and ordained ministry in particular. I had engaged earlier in writing a Covey-style personal mission statement while studying for a leadership module of a MTh, an exercise that had felt very theoretical. Carried out in the midst of burnout it took on a new and very practical relevance. The resulting short statement covers my identity, purpose and roles, expressed in short statements. My roles include husband, father and family member/friend. My ordained role is as 'President—an oversight role,' 'Pastor—a saint-making role' and 'Priest—a representative role,' with bullet points expressing the unique calling I believe I have in relation to each. This statement has become a key tool for planning use of time. But, more importantly, it keeps me connected with who I am and why I do what I do in ministry and my wider life. The hour I spend using this tool at the start of each week has become one of the life-giving disciplines of engagement.

Writing a personal mission statement took on a new and very practical relevance

For the Church

In the last decade, the Church of England has worked its way through a process of clarification in relation to clergy terms and conditions in preparation for the Ecclesiastical Offices (Terms of Service) Legislation. This process offers much actual and potential positive fruit already in relation to some of the issues touched on in this booklet. For example, two key requirements are for Ministry Development Review and the framing of Role Descriptions. In their Grove booklet, *Employed by God?* (Grove Pastoral booklet P 114), Nigel Rooms and Jane Steen explore how ministerial review and continued development could enable these changes to have a positive impact on the practice of ministry.

Over the past twenty-five years virtually all dioceses in the Church of England have created Ministerial Review schemes of different sorts. Mostly they have been administrative reviews with a strong focus on competencies and skills-based CME. The Ministerial Development Review (MDR) envisaged by the new legislation crystallizes the shift towards a more vocational and developmentally-orientated review with an important emphasis on self-review in role. However, it remains to be seen whether this important developmental aim can be achieved through an administrative review.

The MDR involves the development of a Role Description which invites combining the elements of ordinal, personal gifts and experience, and the particulars of context, the same process as Covey's identification of what is truly important. For Covey this is an ongoing and dynamic process. So too such Role Descriptions should not become fixed, but a dynamic tool in ongoing vocational reflection. With the help of well-conducted MDRs, clergy might be stimulated by the church to go beyond what is to what could be as they discover further dimensions of their ordination.

The Roman Catholic Max Thurian expresses what those consequences could and should be in an exciting and stimulating way as he unpacks the term 'ministerial character' as:

> ...this specific relationship between God and his minister, created by ordination, this particular dialogue between Christ and his ambassador, inaugurated by the laying on of hands, this special communication between the Holy Spirit and his messenger, established by the spiritual gift of ministry. This relationship, dialogue and communication remain continuous and living, and must constantly be revived, although they are solidly established between God and the ordained minister, by the sacrament of the laying on of hands.[28]

Preventing and Reversing Ministry Burnout—A Shared Challenge

Ministry burnout can be and must be prevented. Where it has occurred, or aspects of it lurk, steps must be taken not just to alleviate the pain at a superficial level, but to address it at the fundamental level of identity and purpose. Only then is relapse preventable but also the way open to the good for which God works in the midst of burnout once its reality is acknowledged and its potential embraced.

> And we know that in all things God works for the good of those who love him, who have been called according to his purpose. For those whom God foreknew he also predestined to be conformed to the likeness of his Son, that he might be the firstborn among many brothers.
> Romans 8.28–29

That good is rooted in a renewed sense of identity and purpose. Prevention and reversal are the responsibility of both the individual and the church in which they serve, both locally and denominationally, and are, by the grace of God, possible.

Appendix 1: Am I In Danger of Burnout?

These are all feelings and behaviours that are associated with people who are experiencing burnout and also other disorders such as depression or an anxiety-related disorder. This is a simple and informal inventory. It cannot take the place of assessment by a professional. A high score can suggest burnout or another problem that requires professional help.

You can use this tool in two ways—either as a general indicator or as specific to how you are feeling right now. Think about each item. Honestly rate how you have felt at some time in the past or during the past two weeks.

For each question, circle the number from 1 to 6 that best describes you. Then add all your answers for your total score.

1 The extent to which I am feeling negative or cynical about the people with whom I work

1 2 3 4 5 6

Optimistic about parishioners — Cynical about parishioners

2 I enjoy my work and look forward to it regularly

1 2 3 4 5 6

High internal energy for my work — Loss of enthusiasm for my job

3 The extent to which I invest myself emotionally in my work in the parish

1 2 3 4 5 6

Highly invested emotionally — Withdrawn and detached

4 The extent to which fatigue and irritation are part of my daily experience

1 2 3 4 5 6

Cheerfulness, high energy much of the time — Tired and irritated much of the time

5 The extent to which my humour has a cynical, biting tone

1 2 3 4 5 6

Humour reflects a positive, joyful attitude — Humour is cynical and sarcastic

6 The extent to which I find myself spending less and less time with my parishioners

1 2 3 4 5 6

Eager to be involved with parishioners — Increasing withdrawal from parishioners

7 The extent to which I am becoming less flexible in my dealings with parishioners

1 2 3 4 5 6

Remaining open and flexible with parishioners' needs and wants — Becoming more fixed and rigid in dealing with parishioners

8 The extent to which I feel supported in my work

1 2 3 4 5 6

Feeling fully supported — Feeling alone and isolated

9 The extent to which I find myself frustrated in my attempts to accomplish tasks important to me

1 2 3 4 5 6

Reasonably successful in accomplishing tasks — Mainly frustrated in accomplishing tasks

10 The extent to which I am invaded by sadness I cannot explain

1 2 3 4 5 6

Generally optimistic — Sad much of the time

11 The extent to which I am suffering from physical complaints (eg, aches, pains, headaches, lingering colds etc)

1 2 3 4 5 6

Feeling healthy most of the time — Constantly irritated by physical ailments

12 The extent to which sexual activity seems more trouble than it is worth

1 2 3 4 5 6

Sex is a high — Sexual activity is just another responsibility

13 The extent to which I blame others for problems I encounter

1 2 3 4 5 6

Minimal blaming or scapegoating — Others are usually to blame for the malaise I am feeling

14 The extent to which I feel guilty about what is not happening in this parish or with parishioners

1 2 3 4 5 6

Guilt free — Feeling guilty much of the time

15 The extent to which I am biding my time until retirement or a change of job

1 2 3 4 5 6

Highly engaged in my work — Doing what I have to to get by

16 The extent to which I feel used up and spent

1	2	3	4	5	6
High source of energy for my work				Feeling empty and depleted	

Total score (sum of all numbers circled)________

0–32	Burnout is not an issue.
33–48	Bordering on burnout.
49–64	Burnout is a factor in my life.
65–80	You are a victim of extreme burnout. Your life needs a radical change so you can regain your health and vitality.

Appendix 2: What Can I Do?

If you suspect that you are on the road to burnout, seeking help is not something to be ashamed of. It is actually the wise thing to do and the earlier the better. The route you choose will depend on the severity of your own situation and your relationship with your local church and denomination.

The first stop is your family doctor, but make sure it is not your last. He or she may offer an initial diagnosis, medication or other practical help. But possible burnout needs further expert diagnosis and care, reached by referral. Next stop could be a Health Service or independent psychologist or psychiatrist. In addition, in the UK consider advice from the Society of Martha and Mary at Sheldon.[29]

Parallel to this is confidential contact with your denominational authorities. Ideally this is through a dedicated and independent advisor for clergy care. The official route through an archdeacon, bishop or equivalent can be more daunting because of questions about where it leads and what ends up on the record. Now is the time to consider using, reactivating or establishing personal support networks for you (and your family). It is not the time for a 'sticking plaster' solution such as a holiday or a sabbatical.

What is said and to whom in your local church depends on circumstances, starting with trusted colleagues and lay leaders. Initially, in my experience, telling people on a need-to-know basis proved best. If a way ahead involves a noticeable reduction of hours, try to reach a clear agreement stating reasonable expectations. A simple statement to the congregation may be necessary in consultation with local and denominational leadership.

Hopefully expect sympathy and practical help from people you tell. But do not be disappointed or discouraged if you encounter uninformed opinions of what burnout is, because it has become such a slippery, catch-all term. Reactions can range from, 'You've been overdoing it,' advice on how to improve your time management to an implicit but firm message about your perceived personal weakness and to, 'Pull yourself together like we all have to.'

There is a way back up the stairs from the dark cellar called burnout. And it is God who meets you there and who will lead you back.

> A bruised reed he will not break, and a smouldering wick he will not snuff out. Isaiah 42.3
>
> I will give you the treasures of darkness, riches stored in secret places, so that you may know that I am the Lord, the God of Israel, who summons you by name. Isaiah 45.3

Notes

1 *Affirmation and Accountability* (Sheldon: Society of Mary and Martha, 2002).

2 H Freudenberger, *Burnout: the High Cost of High Achievemen*t (New York: Bantam Press, 1980).

3 C Maslach, *Burnout: The Cost of Caring* (Paramus, NJ: Prentice Hall, 1982).

4 http://jmm.aaa.net.au/articles/8275.htm

5 L Francis and D Turton, 'Recognizing and Understanding Burnout Among Clergy: A Perspective from Empirical Theology,' in D Herl and M Berman (eds), *Building Bridges Over Troubled Waters* (Lima, OH: Wyndham Hall, 2004) p 315.

6 C Maslach and M Leiter, 'Reversing Burnout: How to Rekindle Your Passion for Work' in *Stanford Social Innovation Review*, 2005.

7 'Affirmation and Accountability,' Section 1 on church culture and 'From Frustration to Fulfilment,' *Report to the House of Bishops from the Senior Clergy Group Under the Chairmanship of the Clergy Appointments Advisor* (October 2007).

8 The size transition from Pastoral (50–150 members) to Programme (150–350 members) size church is a recognized point for burnout in ministers. See A Rothauge, *Sizing Up a Congregation for New Member Ministry* (New York: Seabury Press, 1983).

9 S Pfeifer, *Stress und Burnout: Verstehen und Bewaeltigen* (Riehen: Klinik Sonnenhalde, 2008) p 18.

10 www.culf.org.uk/files/Clergy%20Stress.pdf

11 'Staying Put—A Look at the First Ten Years of Ministry,' The Alban Institute, Winter 2004.

12 Quoted by D Hicks, 'The Deadly Cycle of Clergy Burnout,' *CMT Newsletter*, September 2008, http://www.liberty.edu/academics/religion/seminary/index.cfm?PID=12850

13 A Gruen, *50 Rituale Fuer Das Leben* (Freiburg: Herder, 2008).

14 H Nouwen, *The Return of the Prodigal Son: A Story of Homecoming* (London: Darton, Longman and Todd, 1994).

15 H Nouwen, *The Inner Voice of Love: A Journey through Anguish to Freedom* (London: Darton, Longman and Todd, 1997).

16 W Friest, 'Understanding and Prevention of Missionary Burnout,' *Taiwan Mission Quarterly*, 1992, http://www.strategicnetwork.org/index.php?loc=kbandview=vandid=4608andfby=2a77d900bedf5585216f23940f5fa79aand

17 Foundational is the agreed role as defined by the denomination or organization, against which calling and development is measured. In the case of Anglican clergy this is to be found in the imperatives of the Ordinal. One of the most creative interactions with the Ordinal is to be found in the *Guidelines for the Professional Conduct of the Clergy*, http://www.cofe.anglican.org/lifeevents/ministry/workofmindiv/dracsc/guidelines.pdf

18 S Croft, *Ministry in Three Dimensions* (London: Dartman, Longman and Todd, 1999) p 155.

19 The Leadership Institute, http://www.tli.org.uk; CPAS http://www.cpas.org.uk/arrow/

20 C Maslach and M Leiter, 'Reversing Burnout: How to Rekindle Your Passion for Work,' *Stanford Social Innovation Review*, Winter 2005.

21 S Cottrell, *Hit the Ground Kneeling* (London: Church House Publishing, 2008) p 25.

22 L Francis and others, 'Psychological Typology of Anglican Clergy in England: Diversity, Strengths and Weaknesses in Ministry,' *International Journal of Practical Theology*, December 2007.

23 http://www.theleadershipcommunity.org

24 R Oswald, *Ending Well, Starting Strong* (Herndon, VA: Alban Institute, 1995).

25 http://www.startingsmartcoaching.com

26 S Covey, A Merrill, R Merrill, *First Things First: To Live, to Love, to Learn, to Leave a Legacy* (New York: Simon and Schuster, 1994).

27 A free online tool for developing a personal mission statement is available at http://www.franklincovey.com/tc/resources/view/msb/

28 M Thurian, *Priesthood and Ministry: Ecumenical Research* (London: Mowbray, 1983) p 162.

29 http://www.sheldon.uk.com/